THE UNSUBTLE ART OF
UN F*CKING YOUR LIFE

A 12 STEPS-INSPIRED JOURNAL FOR SELF-IMPROVEMENT IN MODERN TIMES

A MISFIT MUSINGS OFFERING
BY ANDI WISEMAN

The Unsubtle Art of Unf*cking Your Life
Copyright © 2024 by Andi Wiseman

All rights reserved. No part of this publication may be reproduced, distributed, or transmitted in any form or by any means, including photocopying, recording, or other electronic or mechanical methods, without the prior written permission of the author, except in the case of brief quotations embodied in critical reviews and certain other non-commercial uses permitted by copyright law.

Tellwell Talent
www.tellwell.ca

ISBN
978-1-77941-442-7 (Hardcover)
978-1-77941-441-0 (Paperback)
978-1-77941-443-4 (eBook)

INSTRUCTIONS FOR USE

DO use this journal to:

- ✓ write
- ✓ draw
- ✓ rant
- ✓ reflect
- ✓ give as a gag gift
- ✓ re-gift as a gag gift
- ✓ line a litter box
- ✓ level a wobbly table or chair
- ✓ shred and/or make paper crafts
- ✓ do any harmless joy-sparking things that nurture healing and/or recovery

DO NOT use this journal to:

- ⓧ replace, skip or avoid therapy
- ⓧ replace, skip or avoid medication
- ⓧ depoliticize social issues/inequities
- ⓧ hit anyone (literally or figuratively)
- ⓧ form a cult / promote mob mentality
- ⓧ start uncontained or illegal fires
- ⓧ do any harmful, hateful or otherwise assholey things

DEDICATION

This journal is for anyone whose life feels like if a five-ring circus fucked an explosive trainwreck, resulting in one or more generally unmanageable disasters of incalculable proportions.

It is for anyone who is not only prepared to take personal responsibility wherever and wherever it can be taken, but is also willing to be proactive in making shit right or better and positively changing what can be changed in their life—whatever "what can be changed" subjectively means.

It is for anyone who identifies as being in (or wanting to achieve) "recovery" from something—whatever *that* subjectively means.

It is particularly for anyone who has ever felt dismissed or ignored because their experiences and/or points of view don't fit within popular or dominant practices, beliefs or definitions – especially regarding "recovery."

Most importantly, it is for anyone who desperately needs some goddamn paper to line a litter box or level a wobbly table or chair, and has nothing else on hand.

12 STEPS ("some" not "the")

 admission #1
All the things I actually have choices about in my life are seriously fucked up because of my own shitty behaviours, actions and choices.

 belief
Things are so fucking bad right now I'm willing to hold space for this belief:

"*Change happens regardless, but growth is optional.* With proper help and support, it is possible for me to make different choices and unfuck many if not most of the currently fucked things in my life."

 decision
I resolve to get whatever help and support I can in order to do whatever it is I need to do to unfuck the things in my life I have choices about. I am capable. I am going make positive changes happen in my life. I've already started just by making this decision.

 **reflection**

I resolve to write down all the deeply shameful, fucked-up things I've ever done to myself and/or others, or that have happened as a direct result of my shitty choices, actions and/or behaviours.

For this exercise, I'm also going to **MAKE SURE TO ACCESS CLINICAL SUPPORT** to help me understand the contexts for these fucked-up behaviours and how they developed because of fucked-up shit that happened to me (probably during childhood).

 **admission #2**

I'm going to be brutally honest with myself and at least one other human and share the exact nature of every fucked-up thing I wrote in that reflection exercise from Step #4.

If "spirituality" or a "higher power" authentically resonates with me, I can also choose to honestly share that shit with the god or goddess, ocean, sky, tree, candle, stuffed bear, etc. that is meaningful to me.

I'm also going to make absolutely sure to **CONTINUE ACCESSING CLINICAL SUPPORT** to help me process while I learn to balance accountability for my own actions with self-forgiveness for my previous responses to all the fucked-up contexts I never had any choice about.

openness

I am 100% ready to learn from all these new understandings about how so much shit in my life got so incredibly fucked up.

I am ready to unfuck all the things I have choices about in my life by healthily changing my own thoughts, actions and behaviours.

humility

I acknowledge that every single human in the world—no matter who or where they are—is fighting (often unseen) battles and/or carrying strength and wisdom I know nothing about.

While it's important to cultivate connection, share successes and inspire hope, I will keep judgements and my fucking ego in check. I accept that recovery, health and wellness are subjective; there are literally a million or more paths to achieving them, and aggressively insisting my path is the only path would be a serious dick move.

intention

I am making a list of all the people who have been harmed directly or indirectly by my fucked-up choices and/or shitty actions or behaviours, with an honest willingness to make meaningful amends.

I remember that amends often involve more than just words. Ideally, they are genuinely meaningful for the person to whom the amends are being made and not just the person making them.

I am also going to **CONTINUE ACCESSING CLINICAL SUPPORT** to increase my own awareness about how my own intentions (conscious or subconscious) can and do drive my choices, actions and behaviours.

righting wrongs
When and however possible, I will make direct and meaningful amends to everyone harmed or negatively impacted by my part in whatever fuckery my choices, actions or behaviours caused them, except where to do so would just cause more fuckery or harm.

I will also think about how I can incorporate healthy, appropriate other-centeredness into my day-to-day living, as a way of making amends to my community and the world I live in and move through.

 accountability
I'm staying honest with myself and others, one second, minute, hour, day at a time, in perpetuity

I acknowledge that I'm 100% responsible for my thoughts, actions and behaviours and I will actively do everything I possibly can to keep my life and the lives of others I impact free from destructive fuckery.

sustainability
Understanding that as long as we're alive journeys like these are never "done," I will continue my own learning and self-work.

I will make sure I maintain connections with the supports, networks and resources that are healthy and beneficial for me (including taking prescribed medication, if applicable).

As I humbly move forward with unfucking my own life, I will stay respectful of different journeys and remain open to learning from the (*equally valuable*) perspectives of others who took or are taking different paths to unfuck theirs.

 **pay it forward**

Having come to understand my own shitty behaviours and how they came to be, and using this new understanding to successfully unfuck all the things I have choices about in my life, I resolve to move forward in this world modelling constructive compassion, humility and kindness in all my affairs.

I know I can continue to **ACCESS CLINICAL SUPPORT** any time life and/or situations become overwhelming or difficult to manage. I know there is absolutely no shame in getting help and support for my own mental health and emotional wellness—ever.

And since pain plus time equals comedy, a bit of fucking humour here and there never hurt either!

WRITE IT OUT

Grab some pens and get ready to kick it old-school! When we're trying to learn and/or remember things, putting pen to paper is more effective than typing in a digital format. Also, personal journalling strengthens our ability to cope with the unrelenting fuckery-induced stressors in our uniquely personal day-to-day grind. This is 100% for-actual-real science.

And not science like "*my racist great-aunt saw some online videos about how everything all those so-called scientists say is actually fake science and that's why so-called facts are also totally fake, because the elitist puppets in charge don't want you to know about Pizzagate or the Lizard People controlling everything,*" either.

The mental health benefits of journaling with a pen on paper have been proven through something called "objectively evidenced science," the kind that will ultimately withstand any (often hysterical/histrionic) annihilations of critical-thinking that large populaces of humanity seem to be experiencing at the moment.

So, let your mind and emotions flow through the writing instruments of your choice as you gently dip your cognitive toes into your most pressing personal shitstorms. "The only way out is through," as the saying goes.

As you move forward, know with certainty that wherever you have any choice, you absolutely can connect with yourself and others, make positive changes and successfully unfuck your life.

And as American writer Richard Bach, author of that 1970's bestseller, *Jonathan Livingston Seagull*, wisely suggested: "Think about all these things once in a while and watch your answers change."

Yay, it's fucking
journalling time!

JOURNALLING IDEAS

DRAW STUFF

SELF CHECK-IN:
today, here & now

- [ ] shit that's good
- [ ] shit that's fucked
- [ ] what i think / how I feel
- [ ] something I'm excited about
- [ ] something new I'm gonna do
- [ ] some shit (or someone) I'm grateful for

STUFF THAT MAKES YOU SMILE OR LAUGH

MORE JOURNALLING IDEAS

STICKERS & SCRAPBOOKY STUFF

STEP-SPECIFIC NOTES

TOTALLY RANDOM & UNSPECIFIC SHIT

ANYTHING YOU FUCKING WANT BECAUSE THERE'S LITERALLY NO WRONG WAY!

Yay, it's time for **some Step-Stuff Thinky-Prompts**

Thinky Prompt re: admission #1
ACTIVITY #1

With words and/or drawings, use the space around the arrows below to highlight the fucked-up shitshow consequences in your life that led you to this pivotal admission.

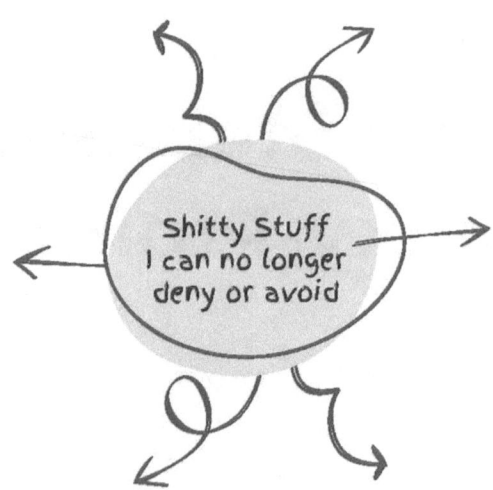

Thinky Prompt re: admission #1
ACTIVITY #2

Getting honest with yourself and admitting just how fucked up things really are is an essential first step. None of us can unfuck anything in our lives without first admitting things are so fucked up that it's probably a good time to properly unfuck them. Congratulations on taking that first step!

With this step, it's very normal to experience all kinds of feelings at the same time. Use the next page to write down and/or illustrate any feelings you've been having as you settle into your own honesty about the fucked-up shit in your life that has to change. Add as many pages as you want or need to.

Remember: you can do this, and you're not alone! **REACH OUT FOR HELP AND SUPPORT IF YOU NEED IT!**

Thinky Prompt re: belief

On the left side of the page, write down five or more reasons you can be confident in your ability to make changes and unfuck your life.

On the right side, write any doubts you might be having. Then call your own bullshit and debunk each one. If this is a bit challenging, think of what you'd tell anyone you love and care about if the tables were reversed.

No doubts? Awesome! Just use this page to celebrate all the confidence you have in your ability to unfuck your life! You totally fucking got this!

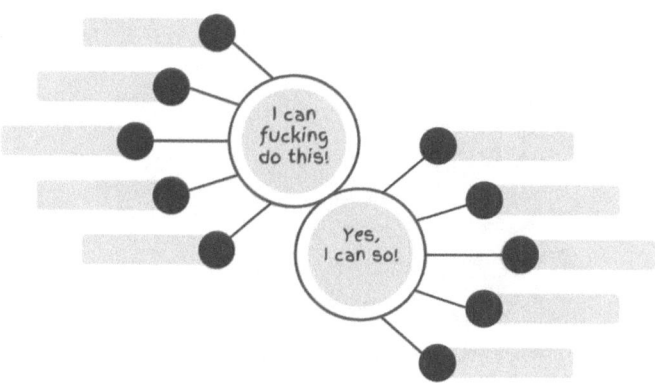

 **Thinky Prompt re: decision**

Woot decision(s)! Now what?

The next couple of pages are intended to help you take a decision and write out a corresponding plan of action, so the unfucking that you want to make a reality is more likely to actually happen.

This basic process can be easily customized to fit any unique specifications your personal unfucking process requires. It can be used for one thing, some of the things or all of the things. Here it is reduced to its lowest terms:

1. Plan the thing
2. Do the thing
3. Achieve the thing

Decisioning Plan Breakdown

1. Identify the fucked-up behaviour or situation you need to change stat, because omfg "unmanageable" doesn't even begin to describe just how fucked it is / things are / you're feeling.

2. Identify the things you can do right now that will start or help start making this change actually happen.

3. Identify the things you need (e.g. resources and supports) to make this change actually happen.

4. Make a "Shit to Do" list, in order of priority, with specific deadlines for each item (so you really for reals do them, because if you don't, you won't be able to make this change actually happen).

5. Determine how you will know that the unfucking process is working, and that change is really happening. What thoughts, actions, behaviours or situations will start to be or feel different?

6. Determine what you can do to effectively prevent whatever you've successfully unfucked from getting fucked up again. What is your emergency plan in case shit doesn't go how you planned or otherwise goes wrong? Who can you call for unconditional support if a slip does happen?

Decisioning Plan Flowchart

Use or make a copy of the flowchart on the next page to write out your action items. Each action item should correspond with one of the numbers listed in the Decisioning Plan Breakdown.

If your action items are numerous or hella complex because the degree of unfucking you're attempting is enormous, use a blank page (or pages) for each number instead of the flowchart box. Then you can art-therapy a nice title page and cover before stapling it all together for ongoing easy reference. Yay, crafts!

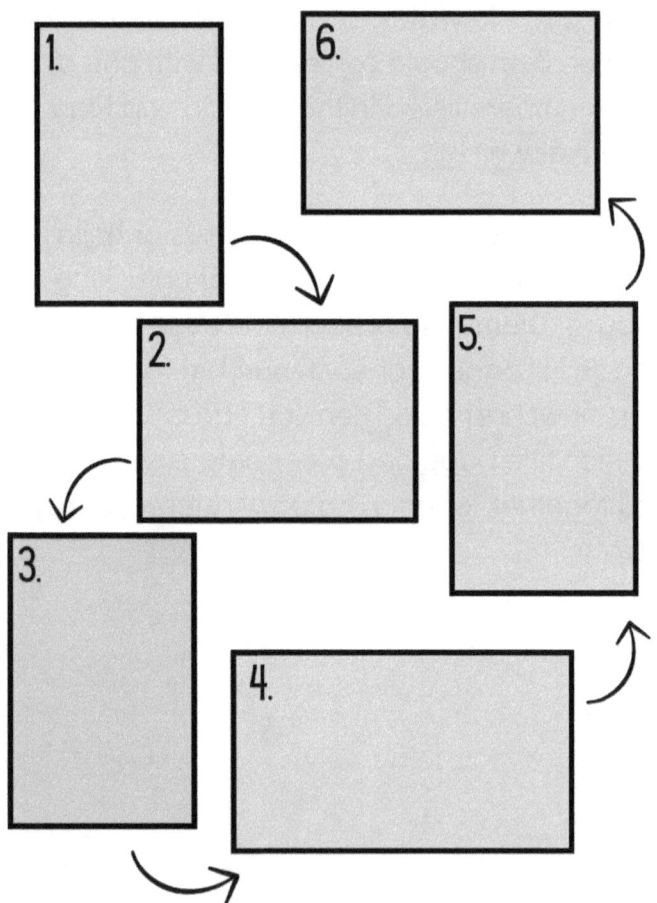

 **Thinky Prompt re: reflection**

This step is an opportunity to reflect honestly on the impacts your harmful fuckery has had on yourself and others.

Focusing on shameful or uncomfortable truths is a notoriously difficult exercise, but it is an essential part of any process that requires honest acknowledgement and accountability. We can be as gentle with ourselves about the consequences we're facing as we can about any of the reasons we avoided or denied them, or for how long.

Remember, it is important to **ACCESS PROPER CLINICAL SUPPORT** before, during and after working on this step. Peer support networks and meetings can be very helpful or even essential complements to clinical care, but are not and should never be considered a replacement for it.

 **Thinky Prompt re: admission #2**

This step is often associated with the idea of "confessing sins," but it doesn't have to be approached that way. Piggybacking on Step #4, this step further strengthens the honesty and accountability we're learning to practice with ourselves and others. The more we practice them - especially regarding our mistakes or struggles—the easier it becomes for them to be foundational in how we think, act and behave in the world.

Remember, it's still very important to **CONTINUE ACCESSING PROPER CLINICAL SUPPORT** while we're learning to balance accountability for our own actions with self-forgiveness for our previous responses to all those fucked-up contexts in our lives that we never had any choice about.

Before, during or after working on this step, do a cost/ benefit exercise.

How much pain, discomfort or anxiety are you feeling about this step? How much fuckery has resulted from dishonesty or avoidance in your life? Now, what are some positive outcomes that you believe honesty and accountability can bring to your life? Think about how it might feel to be free from all the emotional and situational fuckery this step invites you to get honest about, move through and let go.

COST (DISCOMFORT)	BENEFIT (INTEGRITY)

 **Thinky Prompt re: openness**

Have you ever thought about how you actually "know" anything? What about the things that you're absolutely certain about? When was the last time you changed your mind about something?

We all have biases and blind spots. Also, when we've experienced fucked-up things (especially in childhood), our brains are wired to psychologically protect us. Sometimes blind spots or unique cognitive reframes play an essential role in our survival.

This step invites us to stay curious, keep an open mind, and refrain from making judgements—when it comes to ourselves and others, especially when dealing with differences.

Use the next page to list some things you've previously judged or dismissed, that upon further consideration you might be willing to be a bit open or curious about now.

 **Thinky Prompt re: humility**

Humility is essential to our individual capacity to think critically, learn, solve problems and make decisions.

Folks lacking humility are often narcissistic, quick to judge, and exhibit extreme grandiosity when it comes to their own personality, talents, knowledge and opinions. Racism and hatred of foreigners / foreign cultures are examples of the extreme assholery that happens when people lack cultural humility.

How much of a role is humility currently playing in your day-to-day life? Are your levels heathy or do you need some humble pie to bring them up? Take the quiz on the next pages to find out.

Are You Ready to Humble?!

For each of the following statements, circle the letter that corresponds best with the response (listed below) that resonates most with you.

    a. pure, unadulterated 100% agreement
    b. sure, pretty much agree
    c. neither agree nor disagree
    d. don't really agree
    e. couldn't possibly disagree more

1. "Learning is endless?" Fuck that! I already know everything I need to know.
   your answer: a   b   c   d   e

2. Conflicts can be less fucked up to resolve if everyone is willing to compromise.
   your answer: a   b   c   d   e

3. Yeah there's no 'I" in team but whatever - any success I have is mine and mine alone.
   your answer: a   b   c   d   e

4. I'd rather stick sharp shit in my own eye than admit I need help or ask for it.
   your answer: a   b   c   d   e

5. Acknowledging contributions – big or small - from others and giving them credit is extremely important.
    your answer: a b c d e

6. Yeah I'm proud and I boast about shit I've done whenever I can. How else is anyone gonna know?
    your answer: a b c d e

7. Pretending to know shit when you don't is stupid. I'd rather just say I don't know.
    your answer: a b c d e

8. Constructive feedback and learning from others? Yes, Please - I fucking love it!
    your answer: a b c d e

9. If I'm wrong about a thing or if I fucked up, I admit it and do what I can asap to make things right.
    your answer: a b c d e

10. It's not my fault but I really just am better than everyone else, okay?
    your answer: a b c d e

11. Mistakes are a normal part of life and when they happen it's important to learn from them.
your answer: a   b   c   d   e

12. I'll listen but I'm usually right about shit so I just always have the last word.
your answer: a   b   c   d   e

Scoring: a = 4 points, b = 3 points, c = 2 points. d = 1 point, e = 0 points

Results

33 – 48 points
Yay You! Your humility shines bright in a generally naughty world. Be careful though - the lines between "humble" and "doormat" can be very thin. Make sure to keep clear boundaries, because egocentric takers never have any at all and folks with humble, generous hearts are often their favorite targets.

17 – 32 points
With some committed self-reflection, you can be well on your way to making humility a foundation in your life. Stay curious about

other viewpoints, knowledge and experiences that differ from yours, and make an effort to learn more about them without judgements. When listening to others, challenge yourself to really listen – don't just think about things you can or want to say in response. Notice changes that happen when you speak less and listen more.

16 points or less
Very much hope you like humble pie, because it seems you'll be dining on it for quite a while. Clearly, humility is something you need to prioritize improving in your life, because even notorious egomaniac Kanye Fucking West is like *"seriously, mofo? Not even 17 points??"* Successfully unfucking your life cannot happen without genuine humility, so strap in and buckle down! It's definitely time to dive into the education and support you need for cultivating other-centeredness in your life and otherwise getting your colossal ego in check. Yes, we are talking about you. And omfg no, its not a good thing. (insert facepalm here)

 **Thinky Prompt re: intention**

We are never 100% responsible for the reactions or perceptions of others, or their triggers, but approaching things with purposeful intention is still important. Our intentions give us opportunities to align our own actions, choices and behaviours.

When we strive for congruence between what we're thinking, feeling and doing, we have more means for accountability over the choices we're making as we unfuck our life and after.

Whether making amends and unfucking your life or not, it's important to remember the difference between intention and impact.

Use this page to write down some examples of when your honest intentions didn't match the impacts they had, for yourself or for others. Think about anything you might do or say differently today, without compromising any of your own needs or values.

intention

what i wanted to do

how I think & feel

who I am

VS

impact

the reality of my actions

how my actions make others feel

what I did

 **Thinky Prompt re: righting wrongs**

Whether making amends or not, it's always important to actively listen to what others have to say. Let them identify what they want or need (or don't want or need) from you.

This step is about doing whatever you can do to proactively unfuck any shitty impacts you've had on others or in their lives, as long as doing or saying anything doesn't cause any additional fuckery or harm to them or others.

When it comes to the (possibly not so tiny) list of folks you've identified as deserving an apology, some of them are going to have no interest whatsoever in your amends or your offer to make things right.

In fact, some people may be angry that you even reached out, and you might feel angry because "What the fuck? I'm just trying to fucking apologize! How the fuck can I make amends if they won't fucking talk to me?"

In these circumstances, your feelings are valid but their feelings are just as valid as yours. While you're setting about to unfuck your life and take responsibility for stuff, the purity of your intentions does not absolve you from the consequences of all the (possibly more than a few) things you're working to unfuck.

In situations like these, you must do whatever work you need to do to get into acceptance, so you can let it go and move forward. Someone declining your offer to make amends does not diminish your genuine willingness, honesty and accountability, all of which are critical elements of recovery and emotional intelligence. Strengthening them is what will allow you to successfully unfuck your life:

→ **acceptance:** of what happened, of fault (even if it's shared and others aren't taking equal responsibility for their part) and of outcomes

→ **empathy:** with others, with their truths, perspectives and feelings; with yourself and everything you didn't know or couldn't do differently before now

→ **gratitude:** for the openness of others, for the time they're giving you for your process; for whatever happens, even if a continued connection isn't in the cards

 **Thinky Prompt re: accountability**

Personal accountability is one of the non-negotiable ingredients of mature adulthood. We are not responsible for whatever (insert here your personally applicable degree of) fuckery we survived in childhood, but as adults we are 100% responsible for ourselves and everything we have choices about.

This is not to say that larger systems beyond our control aren't impacting our lives—shitty laws, inequitable policies and corrupt institutions can, and absolutely DO, wreak devastating harms across communities, sometimes for generations (just ask Indigenous folks). Few of us can choose the circumstances we live in or the menu of choices we have at any given moment, but all of us are ultimately and eventually responsible for how we play the cards life dealt us, fair or not.

If our skin, gender, sexual identity, socioeconomic status and/or our genetic lineage gives us any measure of privileged advantages and opportunities denied to so many, ideally we can acknowledge the fact. Those with privilege didn't necessarily choose it, but having it likely affords broader opportunities to learn from, listen to and give meaningful support to (the relative majority of) fellow humans still fighting for all manner of equity crumbs in a generally unjust world.

On the next page is an example of a reward chart you can use while you're re-conditioning yourself to practice accountability in everything you do. Connect with an accountability partner and you can help each other as you stay on this new track to keeping your life as fuckery-free as possible.

Define the goal. Keep it small, realistic and achievable (i.e. "I will do - or not do, or do less of - this thing/behaviour every day for the next 7 days." Or "*By subjective and reasonable timeframe of your choice* I will complete *this big or small task.*")

Track your success (i.e. stickers for each day you kick ass with your goals!).

Reward yourself (i.e. treat yourself, in moderation and not with anything that will harm you or others, or negate any of the hard work you've done to get here).

colouring break!

 **Thinky Prompt re: sustainability**

There are literally countless paths to health, wellness, healing and recovery, so it only ever matters that you take the paths that are meaningful and effective for you.

Even if a path you took worked for a while but then didn't, all you have to do is change your direction. There are no "right" paths and no one's journey is "better" than anyone else's. Don't be the asshole running around insisting that everyone else's path is wrong. Instead, keep your eyes on your own prize— whatever that is—and if along the way you're lucky enough to meet someone whose path is different than yours, take the opportunity to share and learn with and from each other.

Because at the end of the day, regardless of who, when or where we are, every human wants and needs pretty much the same basic things: connection, safety and love. These are the basic things that will sustain our recovery – and our lives – long-term.

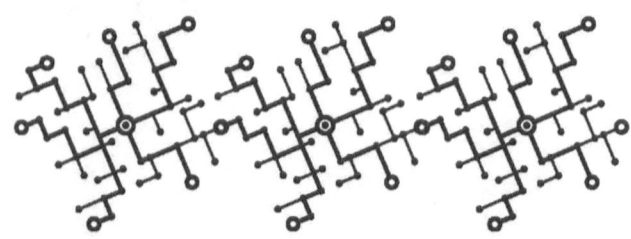

 **Thinky Prompt re: pay it forward**

All this step is about is adding positivity and kindness to the world. Or if we can't do that, we can at least choose to not be an asshole, even if (when) we're being provoked or are otherwise thoroughly fucking correct about something. The energy we have for giving a fuck about things is finite, and we need to be mindful about how and when—and for whom or what—we spend that energy.

There are douchesnozzles everywhere who have yet to do the work you've done to unfuck your life, and they are clearly still crashing their trainwreck selves through the world, leaving all manner of fuckery in their wake. Whether they end up unfucking their life or not, you have worked very hard to unfuck yours so do not let their asshole behaviour destroy everything you've accomplished.

The world desperately needs less assholery and fuckery in it, so pay your integrity and serenity forward not only though service and kindness to others, but by taking the higher road every chance you get. It's not only way more peaceful up there, but as long as you stay true to the steps you took along the way, your paths will lead you to new blessings and experiences you couldn't possibly have even dreamed of before

You've worked so hard to unfuck your own life, and you absolutely deserve every new and unimagined dream your new fuckery-free life can and will bring true. For reals.

Crisis & Mental Health Support

If you or someone you know is experiencing emotional distress or is at risk of self-harm, **immediate and confidential help is available 24 hours a day, 7 days a week.**

In Canada, call 1-833-456-4566

Anywhere else in the world, visit www.findahelpline.com for numbers you can call

If you're in immediate danger or need urgent medical support, call 911.

Overdose Prevention

Canada: call toll-free 1-877-696-1996. Peer operators are available 24-hours a day, 7 days a week, 365 days a year. No stigma. No judgment. www.neverusealone.com

USA: www.harmreduction.org/resource-center/ harm-reduction-near-you

Anywhere else in the world: search "find harm reduction services near me" for numbers you can call and websites you can connect with for information and support.

FREE APPs

Brave App connects people who use drugs alone with anonymous remote supervision: www.brave.coop/overdose-detection-system

Lifeguard App directly links people to emergency responders if an overdose does occur:

www.lifeguarddh.com/products/lifeguard-app

Some Other Variations on the traditional 12-Step Recovery Module

(not an exhaustive list – have fun discovering others!)

Native American 12 Steps	www.youngwarriors.net/static/pdf/resources/sacred_teachings/alcoholics_anonymous_12_steps.pdf
Medicine Wheel 12 Steps	www.whitebison.org/medicine-wheel-and-12-steps
Women's Way Through the 12 Steps	www.hazelden.org/store/item/2309?A-Womans-Way-through-the-Twelve-Steps
Islamic 12 Steps	www.millatiislami.org/www.millatiislami.org/Welcome/12-steps.html
Jewish 12 Steps	www.thebluedovefoundation.org/wp-content/uploads/2020/07/spirituality-prayer-the-twelve-steps-and-judaism.pdf
Buddhist 12 Steps	www.realisticrecovery.wordpress.com/2009/05/29/a-buddhists-non-theist-12-steps
AA for Agnostics	www.aaforagnostics.com

Three (of *many*) Alternatives to traditional 12-Step Recovery Module

(*not* an exhaustive list – have fun discovering others!)

SMART Recovery: www.smartrecovery.org

LifeRing: www.lifering.org

SOS: www.sossobriety.org

Unconvinced that harm reduction works? Or that it can exist without harming anyone's abstinence-based choices, life or recovery?

LEARN MORE HERE: https://hri.global/what-is-harm-reduction

AFTERWORD

Hi. My name is Andi. I'm the "Misfit" that mused the "Musings" in this thing you may have just flipped or scrolled through.

Maybe you found it to be refreshingly amazeballs in its perspicacity, kind of like anything the late, great comedic genius George Carlin ever spoke or wrote. Or maybe you skimmed it and are all like, *"Good Lord. What a messy pile of hot horseshit salad. Wading through it felt a lot like a torturous eternity in hell, where the author is surely heading."*

Either way, hi! Thanks for being here!

So, some context. I worked Vancouver B.C.'s mental health/addiction frontlines in for many years. I served women in the city's infamous Downtown East Side, and from throughout the province. I served women experiencing all manner of complex medical, mental health, and systemic needs. To say nothing of social exclusion, marginalization and vulnerability.

I've seen the "abstinence vs. harm reduction" ("A vs. HR") debate rear as fervently as the "coke vs. pepsi" debate ever did. No one's personal soda preference impacts actual policies and laws, though. So regrettably, the former brings far more real world socio-political consequences.

As omnipresent as Starbucks, the A vs. HR discourse is difficult to avoid. In my working roles, I ended up in these polarized spheres a lot. I would criticize the harms of exiling folks if/when relapses occur. And without exception, someone would insist "we're more progressive and open these days. There's less shaming about relapse."

And I'd always say I was heartened to hear that. It's awesome that "the rooms" have in them less judgy, more open-minded folks. There's no clear evidence, however, that these insistences reflect significant changes in 12-step culture. And so I continue hoping that non-judgy, open-mindedness becomes its tenets, rather than remaining its unicorn exceptions.

Over the years, I've supported hundreds of women who could've used such open-mindedness.

Women like Kate, whose drug of choice was heroin. Her challenges to achieving two consecutive years of abstinence were herculean. She underwent major spinal surgery, a breast cancer diagnosis and two mastectomies. In 2012, she considered treating her chronic pain with medicinal cannabis. In doing so, she knew she faced certain judgement, scorn and dismissal by her peers in recovery. It was a difficult choice to make, but Kate opted for effective pain relief. As expected, she was promptly exiled from her "recovery community." She shared her devastation in losing friendships from what was by then her many years of struggling in her recovery. Luckily, Kate experienced non-judgmental acceptance and belonging through her cannabis dispensary membership. In 2017, her life ended in tragedy when a hit-and-run driver killed her. Until her last breath, Kate was well loved, connected and supported. Her 12-step exile was never rescinded, but her cannabis community honours and remembers her to this day.

Women like the one standing next to a young woman named Bryce, who I met while working at B.C.'s annual Recovery Day event. I was representing the organization I worked for and the programs we offered. Hundreds of people milling around us, we leaned over the table to hear each other. Bryce shared about a recent relapse. For ten years by then, normalizing relapse and reducing shame about it was a daily part of my job. Using one of my go-to phrases, I said, "Be gentle with yourself, Bryce. Seriously - none of us quit the first time." I hadn't seen the woman standing next to Bryce, but she heard ever word I said. She leaned into the space between me and Bryce, and looked me square in the eye. Words dripping with palpable rage, she said, "Great. You just said I'm gonna relapse." As it turned out, this young woman had achieved two weeks of abstinence at that point. She was living in the same recovery home as Bryce, and Bryce was her designated "buddy" for the weekend. She stomped off, looking not only as though I'd handed her a death sentence, but as though I actually had the power to do so. Her trail of resentment filled my ears and heart and I felt like absolute shit.

It's been more than ten years since that happened. I still feel like shit that my words could hurt someone so vulnerable. If I had known she was listening to my conversation with Bryce, I would've chosen different words. Regardless, I despair that in that situation she believed my words could have that (or any) degree of power.

I always was and remain most infuriated by the 12-step notions that have reduced "recovery" to "this many days 'clean.'" I've said it for years, and I'll say it again. "um, it's a bit more fucking complicated than that, actually." (Learn more by googling "social determinants of health" and "systemic and structural racism").

For many years I prioritized my own job security and toed the standard "recovery" line. I wrote a rant, posted it on my personal social media and website[1]. After over a decade of withholding the fact, I outed myself as someone who identifies as being in recovery from addiction. (A prevailing 12-step belief is that any use of alcohol or drugs ends any

---

[1] Wiseman, A. (2020.). The Recovery Rant. https://www.misfitmusings.com/ranty-opinions-/recovery-rant-intro

recovery achieved prior to that use. As I don't practice abstinence, my recovery isn't generally recognized as such.)

I doubled-down in my insistence that abstinence- and harm-reduction practices can co-exist. I advocated ad nauseam for equal systemic investment in both. I earned my own exile from entire sectors in the process. "12-step traditionalists" are no more interested in considering the life-saving merits of clean needles and safe supply than harm reduction ideologues are in admitting that 100% abstinence is and can be just as important and life-saving in its own right.

And then fentanyl hit. And at the time of this writing, we're now ten years into "the opioid crisis" and unprecedented drug-overdose-related deaths all over every place. With even voting-classes being affected, governments everywhere are predictably "caring." In many places, there's been more state investment in select harm reduction initiatives than ever before. That said, in Canada alone 21 people a day continue dying from preventable toxic drug deaths. Global hullabaloo aside, the "A vs. HR" debates remain as polarized as ever.

(And yes, you best believe there continues to be massive pushback from NIMBYs and abstinence proponents to any and every HR initiative that rolls out in any given community.)

So when I wrote this thing you're holding in your hands, I was thinking of the global toxic drug crisis, and all the hundreds of thousands of preventable deaths that happen everywhere while governments curry election promises and favors alike, and the A vs. HR "debates" roar on. I was thinking of Kate and that woman from Recovery Day.. And all the hundreds of women I've spoken with and supported over the years. I saw so many become lightning rods for judgement, shame and exile from their peers in recovery. So many struggled with an impossible choice between their own authentic wellness and community. Or, fearing exile and shame, I saw many who simply became paralyzed in self-censorship and suppression of their own authentic selves.

These are the women I was thinking of when I wrote this – all the too many I know, and all those I don't know but can well imagine. This I know for certain: many of the women I do know did not survive the shaming and exile they reported or feared.

So here's to survival, healing and "recovery," in all the ways, and for all humans. With unconditional compassion, how about? #ManyPaths

Andi (aka: "the Misfit")
2 December 2023

GRATITUDE & ACKNOWLEDGMENTS

Firstly, this "self-published" book wouldn't have happened without the support and experty know-hows of the good folks at Tellwell Publishing. Alyza, Mitchel, Caitlin, Lara, Bert and Gerardo, thank you for your diligent patience with me, my odd little manuscript, and narrow design visions.

I remain grateful every day of my life for the profound intricacies between nature and nurture that allowed irreverent humour to infuse itself into my baseline way of being and seeing. Humour - the darker, the better - has always mitigated the (often spectacular) fuckery with which my life has also for whatever reasons otherwise endowed me.

To Harmony – without hesitation I would go through every bit of the fuckery that happened in my life before you were born all over again, because the world needs you in it and I love being your proudest Mommy ever.

To Mikey, Kerry and all my chosen family, near and far (you know who you are) – I am grateful always for the safety I have with each of you to embrace my authentic self, and for the non-judgemental love I always receive every time I invariably squeeze her to death.

And last and least, to everyone who, dismissing me and/or my truths, ever said I can't, couldn't or shouldn't be saying, thinking or doing the various "unacceptable" things I've always said, thought and done in my life (you know who you are) – I have black-belt grade survival chops because of your abuse and toxicity in my life. With 100% of my love, respect and gratitude, you can each fuck all the way off.

www.ingramcontent.com/pod-product-compliance
Lightning Source LLC
LaVergne TN
LVHW042001060526
838200LV00041B/1811